I Am Dragonfly Declarations

A 365-Day Journey of
Transformation, Faith, and Becoming

Tammy Corwin

Words Matter Publishing
P.O. Box 1190
Decatur, Il 62525
www.wordsmatterpublishing.com

ISBN 13: 978-1-968542-24-5

Library of Congress Catalog Card Number: 2026933624

Dedication

This book is dedicated to all who feel forgotten in the transformation process—to those who are still waiting, still healing, still becoming.

To the ones who feel unseen in the quiet seasons, who wonder if their prayers are heard, who are tired of trying yet refuse to give up.

To those walking through uncertainty, loss, grief, or change, who feel stuck between who they were and who they are becoming, this is for you.

May these pages remind you that God is still working, even when you cannot see it, that transformation is not rushed, and that you have never been overlooked or abandoned.

You are not behind.
You are not forgotten.
You are becoming.

FOREWORD

The Journey of Becoming

Transformation does not happen all at once.

It unfolds quietly — layer by layer, season by season — just like the dragonfly.

The dragonfly begins life unseen beneath the water, growing in stillness long before it ever takes flight. When the time is right, it rises, sheds what once held it, and emerges transformed — light, strong, and free.

This devotional was written for those moments of becoming.

Each day invites you to declare truth over your life, to align your heart with God's Word, and to step more fully into who He created you to be. These are not empty affirmations. They are scripture-anchored declarations — reminders of identity, healing, purpose, endurance, and eternal hope.

As you journey through these 365 days, may you discover that transformation is not something you chase — it is something God lovingly works within you.

You are becoming.
You are rising.
You are flying.

Welcome to the journey.

AUTHOR'S NOTE

This book was born from a simple truth placed on my heart:

Transformation is sacred.

Life has a way of refining us — through joy, loss, waiting, healing, and surrender. In every season, God remains faithful, gently shaping us into who we were always meant to become.

The dragonfly became a symbol of that truth for me — a reminder that what once felt hidden, broken, or unfinished was never wasted. God was working. He always is.

Each affirmation in this book begins with the same declaration:

I AM DRAGONFLY.

Because identity matters.
What we speak over ourselves matters.
And God's Word is the foundation that holds it all together.

My prayer is that this devotional becomes a companion — something you return to daily, season after season — not just for inspiration, but for grounding, healing, and truth.

May it remind you who you are.
May it strengthen you when you are weary.
And may it point you, always, back to God.

You were created to rise.

SECTION I

Identity & Creation

Who God says I am

Day 1

Affirmation:

I AM DRAGONFLY, created new in Christ, leaving behind what was and embracing the transformed life God has given me.

Scripture:

"Therefore, if anyone is in Christ, the new creation has come: The old has gone, the new is here!"

— 2 Corinthians 5:17 (NIV)

____

____

____

____

Day 2

Affirmation:

I AM DRAGONFLY, fearfully and wonderfully made by God, crafted with intention, care, and divine purpose.

Scripture:

"I praise you because I am fearfully and wonderfully made; your works are wonderful, I know that full well."

— Psalm 139:14 (NIV)

____

____

____

____

Day 3

Affirmation:

I AM DRAGONFLY, rising beyond my past and pressing forward into the future God has prepared for me.

Scripture:

"Forgetting what is behind and straining toward what is ahead, I press on toward the goal…"

— Philippians 3:13–14 (NIV)

Day 4

Affirmation:

I AM DRAGONFLY, transformed daily as God renews my mind, reshapes my thinking, and aligns my heart with His truth.

Scripture:

"Do not conform to the pattern of this world, but be transformed by the renewing of your mind."

— Romans 12:2 (NIV)

Day 5

Affirmation:

I AM DRAGONFLY, called out of darkness and invited to live fully in God's marvelous and life-giving light.

Scripture:

"But you are a chosen people… that you may declare the praises of him who called you out of darkness into his wonderful light."

— 1 Peter 2:9 (NIV)

____

____

____

____

Day 6

Affirmation:

I AM DRAGONFLY, walking in freedom, no longer bound by fear, shame, or the weight of yesterday.

Scripture:

"It is for freedom that Christ has set us free."

— Galatians 5:1 (NIV)

____

____

____

____

Day 7

Affirmation:

I AM DRAGONFLY, healed and restored by the Lord, who gently binds my wounds and renews my spirit.

Scripture:

"He heals the brokenhearted and binds up their wounds."

— *Psalm 147:3 (NIV)*

Day 8

Affirmation:

I AM DRAGONFLY, led by the Spirit of God, walking confidently in truth and direction.

Scripture:

"For those who are led by the Spirit of God are the children of God."

— *Romans 8:14 (NIV)*

Day 9

Affirmation:

I AM DRAGONFLY, strengthened by hope and lifted by God's power to rise above every challenge.

Scripture:

"But those who hope in the Lord will renew their strength. They will soar on wings like eagles."

— Isaiah 40:31 (NIV)

____

____

____

____

Day 10

Affirmation:

I AM DRAGONFLY, known by name, chosen by God, and never forgotten.

Scripture:

"I have called you by name; you are mine."

— Isaiah 43:1 (NIV)

____

____

____

____

Day 11

Affirmation:

I AM DRAGONFLY, alive in Christ, awakened to new life through His grace and mercy.

Scripture:

"Even when we were dead in transgressions, God made us alive with Christ."

— Ephesians 2:4–5 (NIV)

____

____

____

____

Day 12

Affirmation:

I AM DRAGONFLY, walking in God's peace, guarded in heart and mind by His presence.

Scripture:

"And the peace of God, which transcends all understanding, will guard your hearts and your minds in Christ Jesus."

— Philippians 4:7 (NIV)

____

____

____

____

Day 13

Affirmation:

I AM DRAGONFLY, strengthened by Christ to face every moment with courage and faith.

Scripture:

"I can do all this through him who gives me strength."

— Philippians 4:13 (NIV)

____

____

____

____

Day 14

Affirmation:

I AM DRAGONFLY, rooted deeply in love, growing strong and secure in God's care.

Scripture:

"And I pray that you, being rooted and established in love…"

— Ephesians 3:17 (NIV)

____

____

____

____

Day 15

Affirmation:

I AM DRAGONFLY, becoming more fully who God created me to be, walking confidently in His design.

Scripture:

"For we are God's handiwork, created in Christ Jesus to do good works…"

— Ephesians 2:10 (NIV)

____

____

____

____

Day 16

Affirmation:

I AM DRAGONFLY, no longer defined by my past, choosing to live fully in the new work God is doing within me.

Scripture:

"Forget the former things; do not dwell on the past."

— Isaiah 43:18 (NIV)

____

____

____

____

Day 17

Affirmation:

I AM DRAGONFLY, clothed in strength and dignity, facing the future with confidence rooted in God.

Scripture:

"She is clothed with strength and dignity; she can laugh at the days to come."

— Proverbs 31:25 (NIV)

Day 18

Affirmation:

I AM DRAGONFLY, secure in God's unfailing love, resting in His presence and care.

Scripture:

"The Lord your God is with you… he will rejoice over you with singing."

— Zephaniah 3:17 (NIV)

Day 19

Affirmation:

I AM DRAGONFLY, walking in truth that brings freedom, clarity, and peace to my life.

Scripture:

"Then you will know the truth, and the truth will set you free."

— John 8:32 (NIV)

____

____

____

____

Day 20

Affirmation:

I AM DRAGONFLY, strong even in weakness, sustained by God's sufficient grace.

Scripture:

"My grace is sufficient for you, for my power is made perfect in weakness."

— 2 Corinthians 12:9 (NIV)

____

____

____

____

Day 21

Affirmation:

I AM DRAGONFLY, held securely in God's hands, protected by His promise and power.

Scripture:

"No one will snatch them out of my hand."

—John 10:28 (NIV)

____

____

____

____

Day 22

Affirmation:

I AM DRAGONFLY, learning to walk by faith, trusting God beyond what I can see.

Scripture:

"For we live by faith, not by sight."

— 2 Corinthians 5:7 (NIV)

____

____

____

____

Day 23

Affirmation:

I AM DRAGONFLY, planted in God's presence, growing steadily and flourishing in His timing.

Scripture:

"Those who are planted in the house of the Lord shall flourish."

— Psalm 92:13 (NIV)

____

____

____

____

Day 24

Affirmation:

I AM DRAGONFLY, chosen for this moment, placed intentionally by God for His purpose.

Scripture:

"And who knows but that you have come to your royal position for such a time as this?"

— Esther 4:14 (NIV)

____

____

____

____

Day 25

Affirmation:

I AM DRAGONFLY, strengthened daily by the joy of the Lord, which renews my spirit.

Scripture:

"The joy of the Lord is your strength."

— Nehemiah 8:10 (NIV)

____

____

____

____

Day 26

Affirmation:

I AM DRAGONFLY, guarded by God's peace, secure in heart and mind through Christ.

Scripture:

"And the peace of God… will guard your hearts and your minds in Christ Jesus."

— Philippians 4:7 (NIV)

____

____

____

____

Affirmation:

I AM DRAGONFLY, surrounded by God's favor, walking confidently under His blessing.

Scripture:

"Surely, Lord, you bless the righteous; you surround them with your favor as with a shield."

— Psalm 5:12 (NIV)

Day 28

Affirmation:

I AM DRAGONFLY, refreshed and restored as God leads me beside still waters.

Scripture:

"He leads me beside quiet waters, he refreshes my soul."

— Psalm 23:2–3 (NIV)

Day 29

Affirmation:

I AM DRAGONFLY, free from condemnation, walking in grace and forgiveness.

Scripture:

"Therefore, there is now no condemnation for those who are in Christ Jesus."

— Romans 8:1 (NIV)

Day 30

Affirmation:

I AM DRAGONFLY, confident that God is unfolding His beautiful purpose in my life.

Scripture:

"The Lord will fulfill his purpose for me."

— Psalm 138:8 (NIV)

SECTION II

Renewal & Healing

Restoration of the heart and soul

Day 31

Affirmation:

I AM DRAGONFLY, being renewed day by day as God strengthens me inwardly and restores my hope.

Scripture:

"Therefore we do not lose heart… inwardly we are being renewed day by day."

— 2 Corinthians 4:16 (NIV)

____

____

____

____

Day 32

Affirmation:

I AM DRAGONFLY, filled with hope, joy, and peace as I trust fully in the God who sustains me.

Scripture:

"May the God of hope fill you with all joy and peace as you trust in him."

— Romans 15:13 (NIV)

____

____

____

____

Day 33

Affirmation:

I AM DRAGONFLY, no longer walking in darkness but living fully in the light of the Lord.

Scripture:

"For you were once darkness, but now you are light in the Lord."

— Ephesians 5:8 (NIV)

Day 34

Affirmation:

I AM DRAGONFLY, strengthened in my inner being by the power of God's Spirit within me.

Scripture:

"I pray that out of his glorious riches he may strengthen you with power through his Spirit in your inner being."

— Ephesians 3:16 (NIV)

Day 35

Affirmation:

I AM DRAGONFLY, rooted firmly in truth and love, no longer swayed by fear or doubt.

Scripture:

"Then you will know the truth, and the truth will set you free."

— John 8:32 (NIV)

Day 36

Affirmation:

I AM DRAGONFLY, living under God's grace, released from shame and empowered to live free.

Scripture:

"For sin shall no longer be your master… but under grace."
— Romans 6:14 (NIV)

Day 37

Affirmation:

I AM DRAGONFLY, guided by the Lord in every step, trusting Him to direct my path.

Scripture:

"In all your ways submit to him, and he will make your paths straight."

— *Proverbs 3:6 (NIV)*

____

____

____

____

Day 38

Affirmation:

I AM DRAGONFLY, restored by God's faithful love and healed where I once was wounded.

Scripture:

"The Lord will restore you to health and heal your wounds."
— *Jeremiah 30:17 (NIV)*

____

____

____

____

Affirmation:

I AM DRAGONFLY, standing boldly on God's promises, confident they will never fail.

Scripture:

"For no matter how many promises God has made, they are 'Yes' in Christ."

— 2 Corinthians 1:20 (NIV)

Day 40

Affirmation:

I AM DRAGONFLY, lifted by God's strength when I am weary and sustained when I am weak.

Scripture:

"He gives strength to the weary and increases the power of the weak."

— Isaiah 40:29 (NIV)

Day 41

Affirmation:

I AM DRAGONFLY, resting in God's perfect peace as my mind remains fixed on Him.

Scripture:

"You will keep in perfect peace those whose minds are steadfast, because they trust in you."

— *Isaiah 26:3 (NIV)*

Day 42

Affirmation:

I AM DRAGONFLY, walking in obedience, trusting that God's blessings follow faithfulness.

Scripture:

"If you fully obey the Lord your God… all these blessings will come on you."

— *Deuteronomy 28:1–2 (NIV)*

Day 43

Affirmation:

I AM DRAGONFLY, sheltered and protected beneath God's wings, safe in His care.

Scripture:

"He will cover you with his feathers, and under his wings you will find refuge."

— Psalm 91:4 (NIV)

Day 44

Affirmation:

I AM DRAGONFLY, growing in wisdom and discernment as I seek God's guidance.

Scripture:

"If any of you lacks wisdom, you should ask God."

— James 1:5 (NIV)

Day 45

Affirmation:

I AM DRAGONFLY, confident that God is completing the good work He began in me.

Scripture:

"He who began a good work in you will carry it on to completion."

— Philippians 1:6 (NIV)

Day 46

Affirmation:

I AM DRAGONFLY, called by God, deeply valued, and precious in His sight, secure in His love.

Scripture:

"Since you are precious and honored in my sight… I love you."

— Isaiah 43:4 (NIV)

Day 47

Affirmation:

I AM DRAGONFLY, strengthened through Christ, empowered to face every challenge with confidence and faith.

Scripture:

"I can do all this through him who gives me strength."
— Philippians 4:13 (NIV)

____

____

____

____

Day 48

Affirmation:

I AM DRAGONFLY, sustained each day by God's unfailing mercy and faithful compassion.

Scripture:

"Because of the Lord's great love we are not consumed, for his compassions never fail."
— Lamentations 3:22 (NIV)

____

____

____

____

Day 49

Affirmation:

I AM DRAGONFLY, forgiven, cleansed, and renewed as God restores my heart and spirit.

Scripture:

"If we confess our sins, he is faithful and just and will forgive us our sins and purify us."

— 1 John 1:9 (NIV)

Day 50

Affirmation:

I AM DRAGONFLY, walking daily in grace and truth through the life-giving power of Christ.

Scripture:

"For the law was given through Moses; grace and truth came through Jesus Christ."

—John 1:17 (NIV)

Day 51

Affirmation:

I AM DRAGONFLY, deeply rooted in God's love, growing strong and secure in who He created me to be.

Scripture:

"And so we know and rely on the love God has for us."
— 1 John 4:16 (NIV)

Day 52

Affirmation:

I AM DRAGONFLY, watched over by the Lord, confident that He guards every step of my journey.

Scripture:

"The Lord will watch over your coming and going both now and forevermore."
— Psalm 121:8 (NIV)

Day 53

Affirmation:

I AM DRAGONFLY, walking in the peace Christ has given me, untroubled and unafraid.

Scripture:

"Peace I leave with you; my peace I give you."

— John 14:27 (NIV)

Day 54

Affirmation:

I AM DRAGONFLY, chosen and appointed by God to bear fruit that brings Him glory.

Scripture:

"You did not choose me, but I chose you and appointed you so that you might go and bear fruit."

— John 15:16 (NIV)

Day 55

Affirmation:

I AM DRAGONFLY, guided by God's wisdom as I seek understanding and walk in discernment.

Scripture:

"The Lord gives wisdom; from his mouth come knowledge and understanding."

— Proverbs 2:6 (NIV)

Day 56

Affirmation:

I AM DRAGONFLY, never alone, resting in the promise that God will never leave or forsake me.

Scripture:

"Never will I leave you; never will I forsake you."

— Hebrews 13:5 (NIV)

Day 57

Affirmation:

I AM DRAGONFLY, walking forward without fear, empowered by God's spirit of love and strength.

Scripture:

"For God has not given us a spirit of fear, but of power, love and self-discipline."

— 2 Timothy 1:7 (NIV)

Day 58

Affirmation:

I AM DRAGONFLY, being shaped and prepared by God for His greater purpose and glory.

Scripture:

"Those he predestined, he also called; those he called, he also justified."

— Romans 8:30 (NIV)

Day 59

Affirmation:

I AM DRAGONFLY, held steady by God's faithfulness, confident that His promises never fail.

Scripture:

"The Lord is faithful to all his promises and loving toward all he has made."

— Psalm 145:13 (NIV)

____

____

____

____

Day 60

Affirmation:

I AM DRAGONFLY, stepping fully into the new life God has given me, renewed and restored through Christ.

Scripture:

"Just as Christ was raised from the dead… we too may live a new life."

— Romans 6:4 (NIV)

____

____

____

____

Day 61

Affirmation:

I AM DRAGONFLY, restored by the Lord who is continually doing a new and life-giving work within me.

Scripture:

"See, I am doing a new thing! Now it springs up; do you not perceive it?"

— Isaiah 43:19 (NIV)

____

____

____

____

Day 62

Affirmation:

I AM DRAGONFLY, healed by the Lord, trusting His power to restore every part of my life.

Scripture:

"I am the Lord, who heals you."

— Exodus 15:26 (NIV)

____

____

____

____

Day 63

Affirmation:

I AM DRAGONFLY, strengthened as I wait on the Lord, knowing my hope in Him renews my strength.

Scripture:

"But those who hope in the Lord will renew their strength."
— *Isaiah 40:31 (NIV)*

Day 64

Affirmation:

I AM DRAGONFLY, refreshed and renewed in God's presence, receiving restoration for my soul.

Scripture:

"Times of refreshing may come from the Lord."
— *Acts 3:19 (NIV)*

Day 65

Affirmation:

I AM DRAGONFLY, comforted by God in every trial, never alone in my pain or struggle.

Scripture:

"The Father of compassion and the God of all comfort… comforts us in all our troubles."

— 2 Corinthians 1:3–4 (NIV)

Day 66

Affirmation:

I AM DRAGONFLY, releasing every burden and anxiety to the Lord, trusting fully in His care.

Scripture:

"Cast all your anxiety on him because he cares for you."

— 1 Peter 5:7 (NIV)

Day 67

Affirmation:

I AM DRAGONFLY, renewed inwardly by the Holy Spirit, walking in newness of life.

Scripture:

"He saved us through the washing of rebirth and renewal by the Holy Spirit."

— Titus 3:5 (NIV)

____

____

____

____

Day 68

Affirmation:

I AM DRAGONFLY, strengthened by the peace of Christ, allowing His calm to rule my heart.

Scripture:

"Let the peace of Christ rule in your hearts."

— Colossians 3:15 (NIV)

____

____

____

____

Day 69

Affirmation:

I AM DRAGONFLY, walking whole and restored, no longer defined by brokenness.

Scripture:

"The Lord will bless his people with peace."

— Psalm 29:11 (NIV)

Day 70

Affirmation:

I AM DRAGONFLY, restored by God where I once was wounded, renewed in spirit and soul.

Scripture:

"He restores my soul."

— Psalm 23:3 (NIV)

Day 71

Affirmation:

I AM DRAGONFLY, learning to rest in God's care, receiving the rest He freely gives.

Scripture:

"Come to me, all you who are weary and burdened, and I will give you rest."

— *Matthew 11:28 (NIV)*

____

____

____

____

Day 72

Affirmation:

I AM DRAGONFLY, strengthened each day by God's grace, which sustains and empowers me.

Scripture:

"My grace is sufficient for you."

— *2 Corinthians 12:9 (NIV)*

____

____

____

____

Day 73

Affirmation:

I AM DRAGONFLY, rising above sorrow and hardship, holding firmly to God's promise of joy.

Scripture:

"Weeping may stay for the night, but rejoicing comes in the morning."

— Psalm 30:5 (NIV)

____

____

____

____

Day 74

Affirmation:

I AM DRAGONFLY, walking forward in healing and truth, restored by God's faithful hand.

Scripture:

"You restored me to health and let me live."

— Isaiah 38:16 (NIV)

____

____

____

____

Day 75

Affirmation:

I AM DRAGONFLY, becoming whole in God's perfect timing, trusting His process of restoration.

Scripture:

"He has made everything beautiful in its time."

— Ecclesiastes 3:11 (NIV)

Day 76

Affirmation:

I AM DRAGONFLY, rising each day with renewed strength as God restores my energy, hope, and resolve.

Scripture:

"He gives strength to the weary and increases the power of the weak."

— Isaiah 40:29 (NIV)

SECTION III

Courage, Freedom & Trust

Walking boldly by faith

Affirmation:

I AM DRAGONFLY, anchored securely in hope, steady and confident in God's promises.

Scripture:

"We have this hope as an anchor for the soul, firm and secure."

— Hebrews 6:19 (NIV)

Affirmation:

I AM DRAGONFLY, standing unshaken, trusting God as my rock and foundation.

Scripture:

"Truly he is my rock and my salvation; I will not be shaken."

— Psalm 62:6 (NIV)

(**Day 79**)

Affirmation:

I AM DRAGONFLY, walking forward with courage, confident that God goes with me wherever I go.

Scripture:

"Be strong and courageous… for the Lord your God will be with you wherever you go."

— Joshua 1:9 (NIV)

(**Day 80**)

Affirmation:

I AM DRAGONFLY, trusting the Lord with my whole heart, even when I do not understand the path ahead.

Scripture:

"Trust in the Lord with all your heart and lean not on your own understanding."

— Proverbs 3:5 (NIV)

Day 81

Affirmation:

I AM DRAGONFLY, guided by God's truth, walking steadily under His faithful direction.

Scripture:

"Guide me in your truth and teach me."

— Psalm 25:5 (NIV)

____

____

____

____

Day 82

Affirmation:

I AM DRAGONFLY, protected by the Lord who goes before me and stands beside me.

Scripture:

"The Lord himself goes before you and will be with you."

— Deuteronomy 31:8 (NIV)

____

____

____

____

(**Day 83**)

Affirmation:

I AM DRAGONFLY, strengthened by the joy found in the Lord, which renews my spirit.

Scripture:

"The joy of the Lord is your strength."

— *Nehemiah 8:10 (NIV)*

(**Day 84**)

Affirmation:

I AM DRAGONFLY, walking freely in forgiveness, released from guilt and shame.

Scripture:

"As far as the east is from the west, so far has he removed our transgressions from us."

— *Psalm 103:12 (NIV)*

Day 85

Affirmation:

I AM DRAGONFLY, renewed in mind, body, and spirit as God continues His sanctifying work in me.

Scripture:

"May God himself… sanctify you through and through."
— *1 Thessalonians 5:23 (NIV)*

____

____

____

____

Day 86

Affirmation:

I AM DRAGONFLY, walking confidently in God's plans, trusting His promise of hope and a future.

Scripture:

"For I know the plans I have for you… plans to give you hope and a future."
— *Jeremiah 29:11 (NIV)*

____

____

____

____

(**Day 87**)

Affirmation:

I AM DRAGONFLY, strengthened by God's presence within me, never overwhelmed by the world around me.

Scripture:

"Greater is he that is in you than he that is in the world."
— 1 John 4:4 (NIV)

____

____

____

____

(**Day 88**)

Affirmation:

I AM DRAGONFLY, learning to walk in quiet confidence, trusting God in stillness and rest.

Scripture:

"In quietness and trust is your strength."
— Isaiah 30:15 (NIV)

____

____

____

____

(**Day 89**)

Affirmation:

I AM DRAGONFLY, upheld by God's righteous hand, secure and supported in every moment.

Scripture:

"I will uphold you with my righteous right hand."

— Isaiah 41:10 (NIV)

(**Day 90**)

Affirmation:

I AM DRAGONFLY, stepping forward whole, strengthened, and hopeful, confident in God's continued work in my life.

Scripture:

"May the God of peace himself sanctify you through and through."

— 1 Thessalonians 5:23 (NIV)

Day 91

Affirmation:

I AM DRAGONFLY, walking boldly in the light of the Lord, no longer ruled by fear or uncertainty.

Scripture:

"The Lord is my light and my salvation—whom shall I fear?"

— Psalm 27:1 (NIV)

____

____

____

____

Day 92

Affirmation:

I AM DRAGONFLY, living in true freedom through the Spirit of the Lord.

Scripture:

"Where the Spirit of the Lord is, there is freedom."

— 2 Corinthians 3:17 (NIV)

____

____

____

____

Day 93

Affirmation:

I AM DRAGONFLY, released from fear and adopted into God's family with confidence.

Scripture:

"For you did not receive a spirit that makes you a slave again to fear."

— Romans 8:15 (NIV)

Day 94

Affirmation:

I AM DRAGONFLY, walking in victory through Christ, confident that God has overcome on my behalf.

Scripture:

"But thanks be to God! He gives us the victory through our Lord Jesus Christ."

— 1 Corinthians 15:57 (NIV)

Day 95

Affirmation:

I AM DRAGONFLY, strong and courageous, knowing the Lord my God goes with me wherever I go.

Scripture:

"Be strong and courageous. Do not be afraid… for the Lord your God will be with you wherever you go."

— Joshua 1:9 (NIV)

____

____

____

____

Day 96

Affirmation:

I AM DRAGONFLY, empowered by God's Spirit with strength, love, and self-discipline.

Scripture:

"For the Spirit God gave us does not make us timid."

— 2 Timothy 1:7 (NIV)

____

____

____

____

Day 97

Affirmation:

I AM DRAGONFLY, walking freely without shame, radiant in God's presence.

Scripture:

"Those who look to him are radiant; their faces are never covered with shame."

— Psalm 34:5 (NIV)

Day 98

Affirmation:

I AM DRAGONFLY, strengthened in the Lord, standing firm against every challenge.

Scripture:

"Be strong in the Lord and in his mighty power."

— Ephesians 6:10 (NIV)

$$\boxed{\textbf{Day 99}}$$

Affirmation:

I AM DRAGONFLY, fearless because God is with me, strengthening and upholding me.

Scripture:

"So do not fear, for I am with you."

— Isaiah 41:10 (NIV)

$$\boxed{\textbf{Day 100}}$$

Affirmation:

I AM DRAGONFLY, confident that the Lord fights for me as I rest in His power.

Scripture:

"The Lord will fight for you; you need only to be still."

— Exodus 14:14 (NIV)

Day 101

Affirmation:

I AM DRAGONFLY, overcoming the world through faith rooted in God.

Scripture:

"This is the victory that has overcome the world, even our faith."

— *1 John 5:4 (NIV)*

Day 102

Affirmation:

I AM DRAGONFLY, walking in the authority God has entrusted to me through Christ.

Scripture:

"I have given you authority… to overcome all the power of the enemy."

— *Luke 10:19 (NIV)*

Day 103

Affirmation:

I AM DRAGONFLY, liberated to live fully and boldly in Christ's freedom.

Scripture:

"It is for freedom that Christ has set us free."

— Galatians 5:1 (NIV)

____

____

____

____

Day 104

Affirmation:

I AM DRAGONFLY, holding firmly to hope, confident that God is faithful to His promises.

Scripture:

"Let us hold unswervingly to the hope we profess, for he who promised is faithful."

— Hebrews 10:23 (NIV)

____

____

____

____

Day 105

Affirmation:

I AM DRAGONFLY, flying forward in faith, free from fear and anchored in God's goodness.

Scripture:

"And we know that in all things God works for the good of those who love him."

— *Romans 8:28 (NIV)*

____

____

____

____

Day 106

Affirmation:

I AM DRAGONFLY, choosing to live by faith, trusting God even when the path ahead is not yet clear.

Scripture:

"For we live by faith, not by sight."

— *2 Corinthians 5:7 (NIV)*

____

____

____

____

Day 107

Affirmation:

I AM DRAGONFLY, confident that the Lord is directing every step I take according to His perfect will.

Scripture:

"In their hearts humans plan their course, but the Lord establishes their steps."

— Proverbs 16:9 (NIV)

____

____

____

____

Day 108

Affirmation:

I AM DRAGONFLY, listening closely for God's voice and courageously walking in the direction He leads.

Scripture:

"Whether you turn to the right or to the left, your ears will hear a voice behind you, saying, 'This is the way; walk in it.'"

— Isaiah 30:21 (NIV)

____

____

____

____

Day 109

Affirmation:

I AM DRAGONFLY, walking in loving obedience, trusting that God's commands are given for my good.

Scripture:

"If you love me, keep my commands."

— John 14:15 (NIV)

Day 110

Affirmation:

I AM DRAGONFLY, blessed as I place my full confidence and trust in the Lord.

Scripture:

"Blessed is the one who trusts in the Lord, whose confidence is in him."

— Jeremiah 17:7 (NIV)

Day 111

Affirmation:

I AM DRAGONFLY, fearless because God goes before me, walks beside me, and remains with me always.

Scripture:

"The Lord himself goes before you and will be with you; he will never leave you nor forsake you."

— Deuteronomy 31:8 (NIV)

____

____

____

____

Day 112

Affirmation:

I AM DRAGONFLY, more than a conqueror, empowered by God's love to overcome every obstacle.

Scripture:

"No, in all these things we are more than conquerors through him who loved us."

— Romans 8:37 (NIV)

____

____

____

____

Day 113

Affirmation:

I AM DRAGONFLY, drawing strength daily from the Lord, who is my refuge and support.

Scripture:

"The Lord is the strength of his people."

— *Psalm 28:8 (NIV)*

Day 114

Affirmation:

I AM DRAGONFLY, walking in freedom and self-control through the power of God's Spirit within me.

Scripture:

"For the Spirit God gave us does not make us timid, but gives us power, love and self-discipline."

— *2 Timothy 1:7 (NIV)*

Day 115

Affirmation:

I AM DRAGONFLY, choosing trust over fear, placing my confidence fully in God.

Scripture:

"When I am afraid, I put my trust in you."
— *Psalm 56:3 (NIV)*

____

____

____

____

Day 116

Affirmation:

I AM DRAGONFLY, secure in God's protection, knowing He is my fortress and deliverer.

Scripture:

"The Lord is my rock, my fortress and my deliverer."
— *Psalm 18:2 (NIV)*

____

____

____

____

Day 117

Affirmation:

I AM DRAGONFLY, walking confidently in God's will as He teaches and guides me each day.

Scripture:

"Teach me to do your will, for you are my God."
— *Psalm 143:10 (NIV)*

Day 118

Affirmation:

I AM DRAGONFLY, standing firm in faith, courageous and strong through every season.

Scripture:

"Be on your guard; stand firm in the faith; be courageous; be strong."
— *1 Corinthians 16:13 (NIV)*

Day 119

Affirmation:

I AM DRAGONFLY, trusting God's timing and resting in the assurance that every season has purpose.

Scripture:

"There is a time for everything, and a season for every activity under the heavens."

— Ecclesiastes 3:1 (NIV)

____

____

____

____

Day 120

Affirmation:

I AM DRAGONFLY, committing my life and my ways to the Lord, trusting Him to establish every step.

Scripture:

"Commit your way to the Lord; trust in him and he will do this."

— Psalm 37:5 (NIV)

____

____

____

____

SECTION IV

Purpose & Calling

Living with intention and obedience

$$\boxed{\textbf{Day 121}}$$

Affirmation:

I AM DRAGONFLY, intentionally created by God, designed with purpose and called to walk in the good works He prepared for me.

Scripture:

"For we are God's handiwork, created in Christ Jesus to do good works."

— Ephesians 2:10 (NIV)

____

____

____

$$\boxed{\textbf{Day 122}}$$

Affirmation:

I AM DRAGONFLY, called according to God's purpose, trusting that He is working all things together for my good.

Scripture:

"And we know that in all things God works for the good of those who love him, who have been called according to his purpose."

*— *Romans 8:28*

____

____

____

Day 123

Affirmation:

I AM DRAGONFLY, created to walk faithfully in the good works God prepared in advance for my life.

Scripture:

"For we are God's handiwork, created in Christ Jesus to do good works, which God prepared in advance for us to do."
— Ephesians 2:10 (NIV)

____

____

____

____

Day 124

Affirmation:

I AM DRAGONFLY, chosen and set apart by God, called to reflect His glory through my life.

Scripture:

"But you are a chosen people, a royal priesthood, a holy nation, God's special possession."
— 1 Peter 2:9 (NIV)

____

____

____

____

Day 125

Affirmation:

I AM DRAGONFLY, attentive to God's voice, responding with obedience and trust as He directs my path.

Scripture:

"Whether you turn to the right or to the left, your ears will hear a voice behind you, saying, 'This is the way; walk in it.'"

— Isaiah 30:21 (NIV)

____

____

____

____

Day 126

Affirmation:

I AM DRAGONFLY, fully equipped by God with everything I need to accomplish His will.

Scripture:

"May [God] equip you with everything good for doing his will."

— Hebrews 13:21 (NIV)

____

____

____

____

Affirmation:

I AM DRAGONFLY, committed to living a life worthy of the calling I have received.

Scripture:

"Live a life worthy of the calling you have received."
— *Ephesians 4:1 (NIV)*

____

____

____

____

Affirmation:

I AM DRAGONFLY, faithful with what God has entrusted to me, knowing He multiplies obedience and stewardship.

Scripture:

"Whoever can be trusted with very little can also be trusted with much."
— *Luke 16:10 (NIV)*

____

____

____

____

Day 129

Affirmation:

I AM DRAGONFLY, chosen by Christ to bear lasting fruit that brings honor to God.

Scripture:

"You did not choose me, but I chose you and appointed you so that you might go and bear fruit—fruit that will last."
— John 15:16 (NIV)

Day 130

Affirmation:

I AM DRAGONFLY, serving the Lord with joy, gratitude, and a heart aligned with His purpose.

Scripture:

"Serve the Lord with gladness."
— Psalm 100:2 (NIV)

Day 131

Affirmation:

I AM DRAGONFLY, created to shine God's light, allowing my life to point others toward Him.

Scripture:

"Let your light shine before others, that they may see your good deeds and glorify your Father in heaven."

— Matthew 5:16 (NIV)

____

____

____

____

Day 132

Affirmation:

I AM DRAGONFLY, walking humbly and faithfully in God's will, choosing justice, mercy, and obedience.

Scripture:

"And what does the Lord require of you? To act justly and to love mercy and to walk humbly with your God."

— Micah 6:8 (NIV)

____

____

____

____

Day 133

Affirmation:

I AM DRAGONFLY, strengthened by the faithfulness of God, confident that He will fulfill His calling in me.

Scripture:

"The one who calls you is faithful, and he will do it."
— 1 Thessalonians 5:24 (NIV)

Day 134

Affirmation:

I AM DRAGONFLY, living with purpose and direction, trusting the Lord to fulfill His plans for my life.

Scripture:

"The Lord will fulfill his purpose for me."
— Psalm 138:8 (NIV)

Day 135

Affirmation:

I AM DRAGONFLY, fully aligned with God's purpose, committing my plans to Him and trusting His guidance.

Scripture:

"Commit to the Lord whatever you do, and he will establish your plans."

— Proverbs 16:3 (NIV)

____

____

____

____

Day 136

Affirmation:

I AM DRAGONFLY, created to make a meaningful impact through love, compassion, and faithful obedience to God.

Scripture:

"And now these three remain: faith, hope and love. But the greatest of these is love."

— 1 Corinthians 13:13 (NIV)

____

____

____

____

Day 137

Affirmation:

I AM DRAGONFLY, called to serve others humbly, reflecting the heart of Christ in my actions.

Scripture:

"Serve one another humbly in love."

— Galatians 5:13 (NIV)

____

____

____

____

Day 138

Affirmation:

I AM DRAGONFLY, faithful in both small and great responsibilities, honoring God with my obedience.

Scripture:

"Well done, good and faithful servant!"

— Matthew 25:21 (NIV)

____

____

____

____

Day 139

Affirmation:

I AM DRAGONFLY, living a life that mirrors Christ, allowing His love and truth to shape my character.

Scripture:

"Whoever claims to live in him must live as Jesus did."

— *1 John 2:6 (NIV)*

Day 140

Affirmation:

I AM DRAGONFLY, using the gifts God has given me to serve others and glorify Him.

Scripture:

"Each of you should use whatever gift you have received to serve others."

— *1 Peter 4:10 (NIV)*

Day 141

Affirmation:

I AM DRAGONFLY, walking wisely and intentionally, making the most of every opportunity God provides.

Scripture:

"Be very careful, then, how you live—not as unwise but as wise."

— Ephesians 5:15 (NIV)

____

____

____

____

Day 142

Affirmation:

I AM DRAGONFLY, sowing seeds of goodness and faith, trusting God for the harvest in His time.

Scripture:

"Let us not become weary in doing good, for at the proper time we will reap a harvest."

— Galatians 6:9 (NIV)

____

____

____

____

Affirmation:

I AM DRAGONFLY, living on mission with God, willing to go wherever He leads and serve however He calls.

Scripture:

"Go and make disciples of all nations."

— Matthew 28:19 (NIV)

Affirmation:

I AM DRAGONFLY, committed to walking in integrity and truth, honoring God in every decision.

Scripture:

"The Lord detests lying lips, but he delights in people who are trustworthy."

— Proverbs 12:22 (NIV)

(**Day 145**)

Affirmation:

I AM DRAGONFLY, reflecting God's goodness through my words, actions, and daily choices.

Scripture:

"Let us do good to all people."

— *Galatians 6:10 (NIV)*

____

____

____

____

(**Day 146**)

Affirmation:

I AM DRAGONFLY, confidently carrying out the assignment God has entrusted to me.

Scripture:

"Carry out the ministry you have received in the Lord."

— *Colossians 4:17 (NIV)*

____

____

____

____

Day 147

Affirmation:

I AM DRAGONFLY, motivated by love rather than obligation, serving God with a willing heart.

Scripture:

"Whatever you do, do it all for the glory of God."
— *1 Corinthians 10:31 (NIV)*

Day 148

Affirmation:

I AM DRAGONFLY, shining brightly as a light in the world, reflecting God's presence wherever I go.

Scripture:

"Shine among them like stars in the sky."
— *Philippians 2:15 (NIV)*

Day 149

Affirmation:

I AM DRAGONFLY, faithful to finish the work God has placed before me, enduring with strength and grace.

Scripture:

"I have fought the good fight, I have finished the race, I have kept the faith."

— 2 Timothy 4:7 (NIV)

Day 150

Affirmation:

I AM DRAGONFLY, living a life that honors God and leaves a legacy of faith, love, and obedience.

Scripture:

"In the same way, let your light shine before others."

— Matthew 5:16 (NIV)

Affirmation:

I AM DRAGONFLY, strengthened by God to persevere through every season, running the race He has set before me with endurance and faith.

Scripture:

"Let us run with perseverance the race marked out for us."
— *Hebrews 12:1 (NIV)*

Affirmation:

I AM DRAGONFLY, steadfast and immovable, anchored in my calling and unshaken by circumstances.

Scripture:

"Stand firm. Let nothing move you."
— *1 Corinthians 15:58 (NIV)*

Day 153

Affirmation:

I AM DRAGONFLY, patient in hardship and joyful in hope, remaining faithful as God works through every challenge.

Scripture:

"Be joyful in hope, patient in affliction, faithful in prayer."
— *Romans 12:12 (NIV)*

____

____

____

____

Day 154

Affirmation:

I AM DRAGONFLY, strengthened when I grow weary, choosing to continue doing good with trust in God's timing.

Scripture:

"Let us not become weary in doing good."
— *Galatians 6:9 (NIV)*

____

____

____

____

Day 155

Affirmation:

I AM DRAGONFLY, trusting God in seasons of waiting, confident that He is always working on my behalf.

Scripture:

"Wait for the Lord; be strong and take heart and wait for the Lord."

— Psalm 27:14 (NIV)

____

____

____

____

Day 156

Affirmation:

I AM DRAGONFLY, confident that God faithfully completes every good work He begins in my life.

Scripture:

"He who began a good work in you will carry it on to completion."

— Philippians 1:6 (NIV)

____

____

____

____

Day 157

Affirmation:

I AM DRAGONFLY, enduring trials with faith, knowing God is refining my character and strengthening my purpose.

Scripture:

"Because you know that the testing of your faith produces perseverance."

— *James 1:3 (NIV)*

Day 158

Affirmation:

I AM DRAGONFLY, anchored in a hope that does not disappoint, secure in God's unfailing love.

Scripture:

"Hope does not put us to shame, because God's love has been poured out into our hearts."

— *Romans 5:5 (NIV)*

Day 159

Affirmation:

I AM DRAGONFLY, sustained by the Lord's great love, strengthened even in moments of weakness.

Scripture:

"Because of the Lord's great love we are not consumed."
— Lamentations 3:22 (NIV)

Day 160

Affirmation:

I AM DRAGONFLY, choosing to remain rooted where God has placed me, growing through connection with Him.

Scripture:

"Remain in me, as I also remain in you."
—John 15:4 (NIV)

Day 161

Affirmation:

I AM DRAGONFLY, enduring hardship with courage, trusting God's discipline to shape and strengthen me.

Scripture:

"Endure hardship as discipline; God is treating you as his children."

— Hebrews 12:7 (NIV)

Day 162

Affirmation:

I AM DRAGONFLY, strengthened daily by God's grace, which is sufficient for every need I face.

Scripture:

"My grace is sufficient for you."

— 2 Corinthians 12:9 (NIV)

Day 163

Affirmation:

I AM DRAGONFLY, growing in character and hope as perseverance continues its work in me.

Scripture:

"Perseverance produces character; and character, hope."
— Romans 5:4 (NIV)

____

____

____

____

Day 164

Affirmation:

I AM DRAGONFLY, pressing forward with determination toward the calling God has placed on my life.

Scripture:

"I press on toward the goal to win the prize."
— Philippians 3:14 (NIV)

____

____

____

____

Affirmation:

I AM DRAGONFLY, committed to finishing strong, trusting God's timing and remaining faithful to the end.

Scripture:

"Blessed is the one who perseveres under trial."

— James 1:12 (NIV)

SECTION V

Faith, Endurance & Perseverance

Remaining faithful through every season

Day 166

Affirmation:

I AM DRAGONFLY, trusting God to guide my life with wisdom as I walk faithfully in His purpose.

Scripture:

"Trust in the Lord with all your heart and lean not on your own understanding."

— *Proverbs 3:5 (NIV)*

Day 167

Affirmation:

I AM DRAGONFLY, led by the Lord as I acknowledge Him in every decision and direction.

Scripture:

"In all your ways submit to him, and he will make your paths straight."

— *Proverbs 3:6 (NIV)*

Day 168

Affirmation:

I AM DRAGONFLY, walking confidently in God's plans, knowing they are filled with hope and promise.

Scripture:

"For I know the plans I have for you… plans to give you hope and a future."

— Jeremiah 29:11 (NIV)

Day 169

Affirmation:

I AM DRAGONFLY, resting in God's faithfulness, assured that He never forgets His promises.

Scripture:

"Let us hold unswervingly to the hope we profess, for he who promised is faithful."

— Hebrews 10:23 (NIV)

Day 170

Affirmation:

I AM DRAGONFLY, strengthened by faith as I trust God even when outcomes are unseen.

Scripture:

"Now faith is confidence in what we hope for and assurance about what we do not see."

— *Hebrews 11:1 (NIV)*

Day 171

Affirmation:

I AM DRAGONFLY, walking daily by faith, confident that God orders my steps.

Scripture:

"For we live by faith, not by sight."

— *2 Corinthians 5:7 (NIV)*

Day 172

Affirmation:

I AM DRAGONFLY, anchored in God's Word, finding strength and direction through His truth.

Scripture:

"Your word is a lamp for my feet, a light on my path."
— Psalm 119:105 (NIV)

____

____

____

____

Day 173

Affirmation:

I AM DRAGONFLY, growing in trust as I wait patiently for the Lord's perfect timing.

Scripture:

"Wait for the Lord; be strong and take heart and wait for the Lord."
— Psalm 27:14 (NIV)

____

____

____

____

Day 174

Affirmation:

I AM DRAGONFLY, confident that God strengthens me as I place my hope in Him.

Scripture:

"But those who hope in the Lord will renew their strength."
— *Isaiah 40:31 (NIV)*

____

____

____

____

Day 175

Affirmation:

I AM DRAGONFLY, walking steadily in peace as I trust God's control over my life.

Scripture:

"You will keep in perfect peace those whose minds are steadfast, because they trust in you."
— *Isaiah 26:3 (NIV)*

____

____

____

____

Day 176

Affirmation:

I AM DRAGONFLY, learning contentment through faith, trusting God's provision in every season.

Scripture:

"And my God will meet all your needs according to the riches of his glory in Christ Jesus."

— Philippians 4:19 (NIV)

Day 177

Affirmation:

I AM DRAGONFLY, strengthened to stand firm in faith, even through trials and uncertainty.

Scripture:

"Be on your guard; stand firm in the faith; be courageous; be strong."

— 1 Corinthians 16:13 (NIV)

Day 178

Affirmation:

I AM DRAGONFLY, trusting God to work all things together for good in my life.

Scripture:

"And we know that in all things God works for the good of those who love him."

— Romans 8:28 (NIV)

____

____

____

____

Day 179

Affirmation:

I AM DRAGONFLY, confident that the Lord is my strength and refuge in every circumstance.

Scripture:

"The Lord is my strength and my shield."

— Psalm 28:7 (NIV)

____

____

____

____

Day 180

Affirmation:

I AM DRAGONFLY, firmly established in faith, trusting God to complete His work in my life.

Scripture:

"He who began a good work in you will carry it on to completion."

— *Philippians 1:6 (NIV)*

Day 181

Affirmation:

I AM DRAGONFLY, walking by faith with confidence, trusting God beyond what my eyes can see.

Scripture:

"For we live by faith, not by sight."

— *2 Corinthians 5:7 (NIV)*

Day 182

Affirmation:

I AM DRAGONFLY, placing my trust fully in the Lord, confident that He is my refuge and strength.

Scripture:

"Trust in the Lord forever, for the Lord, the Lord himself, is the Rock eternal."

— *Isaiah 26:4 (NIV)*

Day 183

Affirmation:

I AM DRAGONFLY, standing firm in faith even when circumstances challenge my understanding.

Scripture:

"Now faith is confidence in what we hope for and assurance about what we do not see."

— *Hebrews 11:1 (NIV)*

Affirmation:

I AM DRAGONFLY, strengthened as I place my hope in God, knowing He renews my strength.

Scripture:

"But those who hope in the Lord will renew their strength."

— *Isaiah 40:31 (NIV)*

Day 185

Affirmation:

I AM DRAGONFLY, trusting the Lord to direct my path as I acknowledge Him in all my ways.

Scripture:

"In all your ways submit to him, and he will make your paths straight."

— *Proverbs 3:6 (NIV)*

Day 186

Affirmation:

I AM DRAGONFLY, resting in God's peace as I trust Him with every concern and outcome.

Scripture:

"You will keep in perfect peace those whose minds are steadfast, because they trust in you."

— Isaiah 26:3 (NIV)

Day 187

Affirmation:

I AM DRAGONFLY, strengthened by God's promises, holding firmly to hope without wavering.

Scripture:

"Let us hold unswervingly to the hope we profess, for he who promised is faithful."

— Hebrews 10:23 (NIV)

Day 188

Affirmation:

I AM DRAGONFLY, persevering through trials with faith, trusting God to refine and strengthen me.

Scripture:

"Because you know that the testing of your faith produces perseverance."

— James 1:3 (NIV)

Day 189

Affirmation:

I AM DRAGONFLY, confident that God is working for good in every season of my life.

Scripture:

"And we know that in all things God works for the good of those who love him."

— Romans 8:28 (NIV)

Day 190

Affirmation:

I AM DRAGONFLY, trusting God's timing and remaining patient as His plan unfolds.

Scripture:

"There is a time for everything, and a season for every activity under the heavens."

— Ecclesiastes 3:1 (NIV)

____

____

____

____

Day 191

Affirmation:

I AM DRAGONFLY, standing strong in faith, knowing the Lord is my strength and shield.

Scripture:

"The Lord is my strength and my shield; my heart trusts in him."

— Psalm 28:7 (NIV)

____

____

____

____

Affirmation:

I AM DRAGONFLY, choosing trust over fear, anchored in the faithfulness of God.

Scripture:

"When I am afraid, I put my trust in you."

— Psalm 56:3 (NIV)

____

____

____

____

Day 193

Affirmation:

I AM DRAGONFLY, persevering with patience, confident that God rewards those who seek Him.

Scripture:

"Blessed is the one who perseveres under trial."

— James 1:12 (NIV)

____

____

____

____

Day 194

Affirmation:

I AM DRAGONFLY, strengthened daily by God's grace, which is sufficient for every challenge I face.

Scripture:

"My grace is sufficient for you."

— *2 Corinthians 12:9 (NIV)*

Day 195

Affirmation:

I AM DRAGONFLY, firmly rooted in faith, trusting God to complete the work He has begun in me.

Scripture:

"He who began a good work in you will carry it on to completion."

— *Philippians 1:6 (NIV)*

Day 196

Affirmation:

I AM DRAGONFLY, learning to rely completely on the Lord, whose strength carries me through every challenge.

Scripture:

"My flesh and my heart may fail, but God is the strength of my heart and my portion forever."

— Psalm 73:26 (NIV)

Day 197

Affirmation:

I AM DRAGONFLY, trusting God to sustain me as I wait patiently and faithfully for His direction.

Scripture:

"The Lord is good to those whose hope is in him, to the one who seeks him."

— Lamentations 3:25 (NIV)

Day 198

Affirmation:

I AM DRAGONFLY, strengthened by God's Word, which anchors my faith and guides my steps.

Scripture:

"Your word is a lamp for my feet, a light on my path."
— *Psalm 119:105 (NIV)*

Day 199

Affirmation:

I AM DRAGONFLY, confident that the Lord hears my prayers and responds according to His perfect will.

Scripture:

"This is the confidence we have in approaching God: that if we ask anything according to his will, he hears us."
— *1 John 5:14 (NIV)*

Day 200

Affirmation:

I AM DRAGONFLY, strengthened in spirit as I seek God first and trust Him to provide all I need.

Scripture:

"But seek first his kingdom and his righteousness, and all these things will be given to you as well."

— Matthew 6:33 (NIV)

Day 201

Affirmation:

I AM DRAGONFLY, standing firm in faith, refusing to be shaken by trials or uncertainty.

Scripture:

"Therefore let us be grateful for receiving a kingdom that cannot be shaken."

— Hebrews 12:28 (NIV)

Day 202

Affirmation:

I AM DRAGONFLY, strengthened as I wait on the Lord, trusting Him to renew my strength daily.

Scripture:

"But those who hope in the Lord will renew their strength."
— *Isaiah 40:31 (NIV)*

____

____

____

____

Day 203

Affirmation:

I AM DRAGONFLY, choosing patience and perseverance, knowing God is at work even when I cannot see it.

Scripture:

"Be patient, then, brothers and sisters, until the Lord's coming."

— *James 5:7 (NIV)*

____

____

____

____

Day 204

Affirmation:

I AM DRAGONFLY, strengthened by the peace of God, which guards my heart and mind.

Scripture:

"And the peace of God, which transcends all understanding, will guard your hearts and your minds in Christ Jesus."
— *Philippians 4:7 (NIV)*

Day 205

Affirmation:

I AM DRAGONFLY, confident that the Lord goes before me, preparing the way ahead.

Scripture:

"The Lord himself goes before you and will be with you."
— *Deuteronomy 31:8 (NIV)*

Day 206

Affirmation:

I AM DRAGONFLY, strengthened to endure hardship with faith, trusting God's refining work in my life.

Scripture:

"Blessed is the one who perseveres under trial."

—James 1:12 (NIV)

Day 207

Affirmation:

I AM DRAGONFLY, anchored in hope that sustains me through every season.

Scripture:

"We have this hope as an anchor for the soul, firm and secure."

— Hebrews 6:19 (NIV)

Affirmation:

I AM DRAGONFLY, trusting God to strengthen me from within through His Spirit.

Scripture:

"I pray that out of his glorious riches he may strengthen you with power through his Spirit in your inner being."
— *Ephesians 3:16 (NIV)*

____

____

____

____

Day 209

Affirmation:

I AM DRAGONFLY, persevering with joy, confident that God is faithful to complete His work in me.

Scripture:

"The one who calls you is faithful, and he will do it."
— *1 Thessalonians 5:24 (NIV)*

____

____

____

____

Affirmation:

I AM DRAGONFLY, standing firm in faith, rooted deeply in the unchanging promises of God.

Scripture:

"Stand firm in the faith."

— 1 Corinthians 16:13 (NIV)

SECTION VI

Peace, Wisdom & Discernment

Quiet confidence in God's leading

Day 211

Affirmation:

I AM DRAGONFLY, resting securely in God's peace, knowing He holds every detail of my life.

Scripture:

"You will keep in perfect peace those whose minds are steadfast, because they trust in you."

— Isaiah 26:3 (NIV)

____

____

____

____

Day 212

Affirmation:

I AM DRAGONFLY, calm and untroubled, choosing trust over anxiety as I place my cares in God's hands.

Scripture:

"Cast all your anxiety on him because he cares for you."

— 1 Peter 5:7 (NIV)

____

____

____

____

Affirmation:

I AM DRAGONFLY, strengthened to remain still and confident as God works on my behalf.

Scripture:

"The Lord will fight for you; you need only to be still."
— Exodus 14:14 (NIV)

____

____

____

____

Day 214

Affirmation:

I AM DRAGONFLY, resilient through every storm, anchored firmly in the faithfulness of God.

Scripture:

"God is our refuge and strength, an ever-present help in trouble."
— Psalm 46:1 (NIV)

____

____

____

____

(**Day 215**)

Affirmation:

I AM DRAGONFLY, resting in the assurance that God's strength is made perfect in my weakness.

Scripture:

"My grace is sufficient for you, for my power is made perfect in weakness."

— 2 Corinthians 12:9 (NIV)

(**Day 216**)

Affirmation:

I AM DRAGONFLY, learning to be content in every circumstance through Christ who strengthens me.

Scripture:

"I have learned to be content whatever the circumstances."

— Philippians 4:11 (NIV)

Day 217

Affirmation:

I AM DRAGONFLY, confident that God is my refuge, sheltering me in every season.

Scripture:

"The Lord is a refuge for the oppressed, a stronghold in times of trouble."

— *Psalm 9:9 (NIV)*

Day 218

Affirmation:

I AM DRAGONFLY, choosing peace as I trust God's control over all things.

Scripture:

"Peace I leave with you; my peace I give you."

— *John 14:27 (NIV)*

Day 219

Affirmation:

I AM DRAGONFLY, resilient in faith, standing firm even when circumstances are uncertain.

Scripture:

"Stand firm. Let nothing move you."

— 1 Corinthians 15:58 (NIV)

____

____

____

____

Day 220

Affirmation:

I AM DRAGONFLY, resting in God's presence, refreshed and renewed in His care.

Scripture:

"He makes me lie down in green pastures."

— Psalm 23:2 (NIV)

____

____

____

____

Day 221

Affirmation:

I AM DRAGONFLY, trusting God to guard my heart and mind with His perfect peace.

Scripture:

"And the peace of God… will guard your hearts and your minds in Christ Jesus."

— Philippians 4:7 (NIV)

____

____

____

____

Day 222

Affirmation:

I AM DRAGONFLY, confident that God renews my strength as I place my hope in Him.

Scripture:

"But those who hope in the Lord will renew their strength."
— Isaiah 40:31 (NIV)

____

____

____

____

Day 223

Affirmation:

I AM DRAGONFLY, walking steadily in peace, trusting God's timing and wisdom.

Scripture:

"There is a time for everything, and a season for every activity under the heavens."

— Ecclesiastes 3:1 (NIV)

____

____

____

____

Day 224

Affirmation:

I AM DRAGONFLY, resting confidently in the Lord, knowing He watches over me continually.

Scripture:

"He who watches over you will not slumber."

— Psalm 121:3 (NIV)

____

____

____

____

Day 225

Affirmation:

I AM DRAGONFLY, secure and at peace, trusting God to complete His work in me.

Scripture:

"He who began a good work in you will carry it on to completion."

— Philippians 1:6 (NIV)

Day 226

Affirmation:

I AM DRAGONFLY, growing in wisdom as I seek the Lord and trust His understanding above my own.

Scripture:

"If any of you lacks wisdom, you should ask God, who gives generously to all without finding fault."

—James 1:5 (NIV)

Day 227

Affirmation:

I AM DRAGONFLY, guided by God's wisdom, choosing paths that lead to peace and life.

Scripture:

"The wisdom that comes from heaven is first of all pure; then peace-loving, considerate, submissive."

—James 3:17 (NIV)

Day 228

Affirmation:

I AM DRAGONFLY, learning discernment as God trains my heart to recognize what is right and true.

Scripture:

"Let the wise listen and add to their learning."

— Proverbs 1:5 (NIV)

Affirmation:

I AM DRAGONFLY, walking confidently in God's guidance, trusting Him to direct my steps.

Scripture:

"The Lord makes firm the steps of the one who delights in him."

— Psalm 37:23 (NIV)

Affirmation:

I AM DRAGONFLY, choosing understanding over haste, patience over impulse, and wisdom over fear.

Scripture:

"The wisdom of the prudent is to give thought to their ways."
— Proverbs 14:8 (NIV)

Day 231

Affirmation:

I AM DRAGONFLY, led by peace as I make decisions, trusting Christ to rule in my heart.

Scripture:

"Let the peace of Christ rule in your hearts."

— Colossians 3:15 (NIV)

Day 232

Affirmation:

I AM DRAGONFLY, strengthened by understanding, allowing God's truth to steady my mind.

Scripture:

"Through wisdom a house is built, and by understanding it is established."

— Proverbs 24:3 (NIV)

Affirmation:

I AM DRAGONFLY, walking in quiet confidence, trusting the Lord to fight battles I do not need to fight.

Scripture:

"The Lord will fight for you; you need only to be still."
— *Exodus 14:14 (NIV)*

Affirmation:

I AM DRAGONFLY, guided by God's Word, allowing His truth to light my path forward.

Scripture:

"Your word is a lamp for my feet, a light on my path."
— *Psalm 119:105 (NIV)*

Day 235

Affirmation:

I AM DRAGONFLY, choosing humility and teachability as God continues to shape my heart.

Scripture:

"Where there is humility, there is wisdom."

— Proverbs 11:2 (NIV)

Day 236

Affirmation:

I AM DRAGONFLY, walking steadily in understanding, no longer tossed by confusion or doubt.

Scripture:

"God is not a God of disorder but of peace."

— 1 Corinthians 14:33 (NIV)

Affirmation:

I AM DRAGONFLY, trusting the Lord to instruct and counsel me in the way I should go.

Scripture:

"I will instruct you and teach you in the way you should go."

— *Psalm 32:8 (NIV)*

Affirmation:

I AM DRAGONFLY, discerning what truly matters, choosing what is excellent and pleasing to God.

Scripture:

"So that you may be able to discern what is best."

— *Philippians 1:10 (NIV)*

Day 239

Affirmation:

I AM DRAGONFLY, living with clarity and confidence, trusting God's wisdom to order my days.

Scripture:

"Teach us to number our days, that we may gain a heart of wisdom."

— Psalm 90:12 (NIV)

Day 240

Affirmation:

I AM DRAGONFLY, walking in wisdom and peace, confident that God is leading me well.

Scripture:

"Trust in the Lord with all your heart."

— Proverbs 3:5 (NIV)

SECTION VII

Light, Love & Legacy

Living a life that impacts others

Day 241

Affirmation:

I AM DRAGONFLY, walking as a child of light, reflecting God's goodness and truth wherever I go.

Scripture:

"For you were once darkness, but now you are light in the Lord. Live as children of light."

— *Ephesians 5:8 (NIV)*

Day 242

Affirmation:

I AM DRAGONFLY, shining God's light through love, kindness, and compassion in every interaction.

Scripture:

"Let your light shine before others, that they may see your good deeds and glorify your Father in heaven."

— *Matthew 5:16 (NIV)*

(**Day 243**)

Affirmation:

I AM DRAGONFLY, led by love, allowing God's perfect love to shape my heart and actions.

Scripture:

"And over all these virtues put on love, which binds them all together in perfect unity."

— *Colossians 3:14 (NIV)*

(**Day 244**)

Affirmation:

I AM DRAGONFLY, choosing love over fear, knowing God's love casts out all fear.

Scripture:

"There is no fear in love. But perfect love drives out fear."

— *1 John 4:18 (NIV)*

Day 245

Affirmation:

I AM DRAGONFLY, loving others deeply and sincerely as God has first loved me.

Scripture:

"Above all, love each other deeply, because love covers over a multitude of sins."

— 1 Peter 4:8 (NIV)

____

____

____

____

Day 246

Affirmation:

I AM DRAGONFLY, called to walk in love, following the example of Christ in all I do.

Scripture:

"Follow God's example, therefore, as dearly loved children and walk in the way of love."

— Ephesians 5:1–2 (NIV)

____

____

____

____

Day 247

Affirmation:

I AM DRAGONFLY, sowing seeds of kindness and mercy that will bless generations beyond me.

Scripture:

"Be kind and compassionate to one another."

— Ephesians 4:32 (NIV)

Day 248

Affirmation:

I AM DRAGONFLY, living generously, knowing that what I give in love multiplies in impact.

Scripture:

"Whoever sows generously will also reap generously."

— 2 Corinthians 9:6 (NIV)

Day 249

Affirmation:

I AM DRAGONFLY, reflecting God's heart through acts of mercy, justice, and humility.

Scripture:

"Act justly and to love mercy and to walk humbly with your God."

— Micah 6:8 (NIV)

____

____

____

____

Day 250

Affirmation:

I AM DRAGONFLY, allowing my life to be a testimony of God's grace and faithfulness.

Scripture:

"Let the redeemed of the Lord tell their story."

— Psalm 107:2 (NIV)

____

____

____

____

Affirmation:

I AM DRAGONFLY, committed to leaving a legacy of faith, love, and obedience.

Scripture:

"Choose for yourselves this day whom you will serve… as for me and my household, we will serve the Lord."
— Joshua 24:15 (NIV)

____

____

____

____

Day 252

Affirmation:

I AM DRAGONFLY, investing my life in what is eternal, not temporary.

Scripture:

"But store up for yourselves treasures in heaven."
— Matthew 6:20 (NIV)

____

____

____

____

Day 253

Affirmation:

I AM DRAGONFLY, living in a way that honors God and draws others toward His love.

Scripture:

"Whatever you do, do it all for the glory of God."
— 1 Corinthians 10:31 (NIV)

Day 254

Affirmation:

I AM DRAGONFLY, faithful to shine brightly until the work God has given me is complete.

Scripture:

"Let us not become weary in doing good."
— Galatians 6:9 (NIV)

Affirmation:

I AM DRAGONFLY, confident that my life, transformed by God, will leave a lasting legacy of light and love.

Scripture:

"He who began a good work in you will carry it on to completion."

— Philippians 1:6 (NIV)

____

____

____

Affirmation:

I AM DRAGONFLY, living with hope that is alive and active, grounded in God's promises for today and tomorrow.

Scripture:

"May the God of hope fill you with all joy and peace as you trust in him."

— Romans 15:13 (NIV)

____

____

____

Day 257

Affirmation:

I AM DRAGONFLY, encouraged by the Lord, allowing His strength to renew my spirit daily.

Scripture:

"Be strong and take heart, all you who hope in the Lord."
— *Psalm 31:24 (NIV)*

____

____

____

____

Day 258

Affirmation:

I AM DRAGONFLY, speaking words of life and encouragement that uplift and strengthen others.

Scripture:

"Encourage one another and build each other up."
— *1 Thessalonians 5:11 (NIV)*

____

____

____

____

Affirmation:

I AM DRAGONFLY, choosing hope even in difficulty, trusting God's faithfulness through every season.

Scripture:

"We have this hope as an anchor for the soul, firm and secure."

— Hebrews 6:19 (NIV)

Affirmation:

I AM DRAGONFLY, living as a source of encouragement, reflecting Christ's compassion and care.

Scripture:

"Therefore encourage one another with these words."

— 1 Thessalonians 4:18 (NIV)

Affirmation:

I AM DRAGONFLY, planting seeds of faith that will grow beyond my lifetime.

Scripture:

"One generation commends your works to another; they tell of your mighty acts."

— Psalm 145:4 (NIV)

Affirmation:

I AM DRAGONFLY, committed to leaving a legacy rooted in hope, truth, and love.

Scripture:

"A good person leaves an inheritance for their children's children."

— Proverbs 13:22 (NIV)

Affirmation:

I AM DRAGONFLY, strengthening others by pointing them toward God's faithfulness.

Scripture:

"Let us consider how we may spur one another on toward love and good deeds."

— Hebrews 10:24 (NIV)

Affirmation:

I AM DRAGONFLY, hopeful and confident that God is still working in every generation.

Scripture:

"The Lord is faithful to all his promises and loving toward all he has made."

— Psalm 145:13 (NIV)

Affirmation:

I AM DRAGONFLY, choosing encouragement over criticism, speaking grace into every situation.

Scripture:

"Do not let any unwholesome talk come out of your mouths, but only what is helpful for building others up."
— *Ephesians 4:29 (NIV)*

Day 266

Affirmation:

I AM DRAGONFLY, carrying hope into places of weariness and despair.

Scripture:

"Praise be to the God… who has given us new birth into a living hope."
— *1 Peter 1:3 (NIV)*

Affirmation:

I AM DRAGONFLY, trusting God to use my faithfulness to inspire those who come after me.

Scripture:

"Those who trust in the Lord are like Mount Zion, which cannot be shaken."

— Psalm 125:1 (NIV)

Day 268

Affirmation:

I AM DRAGONFLY, walking confidently knowing my obedience today shapes tomorrow's testimony.

Scripture:

"Let us not become weary in doing good."

— Galatians 6:9 (NIV)

Day 269

Affirmation:

I AM DRAGONFLY, living as a reminder that God's promises endure through every generation.

Scripture:

"The Lord's love is with those who fear him, and his righteousness with their children's children."

— Psalm 103:17 (NIV)

____

____

____

____

Day 270

Affirmation:

I AM DRAGONFLY, hopeful and confident that the legacy I leave will point others to God's light.

Scripture:

"Let your light shine before others."

— Matthew 5:16 (NIV)

____

____

____

____

Affirmation:

I AM DRAGONFLY, faithful in every season, choosing obedience and trust as I walk with God daily.

Scripture:

"Now it is required that those who have been given a trust must prove faithful."

— 1 Corinthians 4:2 (NIV)

Affirmation:

I AM DRAGONFLY, living with an eternal perspective, setting my heart on things above.

Scripture:

"Set your minds on things above, not on earthly things."

— Colossians 3:2 (NIV)

(**Day 273**)

Affirmation:

I AM DRAGONFLY, choosing perseverance so that I may fully receive what God has promised.

Scripture:

"You need to persevere so that when you have done the will of God, you will receive what he has promised."

— *Hebrews 10:36 (NIV)*

____

____

____

____

(**Day 274**)

Affirmation:

I AM DRAGONFLY, pressing forward with purpose, keeping my eyes fixed on Jesus.

Scripture:

"Let us fix our eyes on Jesus, the pioneer and perfecter of faith."

— *Hebrews 12:2 (NIV)*

____

____

____

____

(**Day 275**)

Affirmation:

I AM DRAGONFLY, finishing the race set before me with faith, endurance, and joy.

Scripture:

"I have fought the good fight, I have finished the race, I have kept the faith."

— *2 Timothy 4:7 (NIV)*

(**Day 276**)

Affirmation:

I AM DRAGONFLY, living intentionally, knowing my time and purpose are held by God.

Scripture:

"Teach us to number our days, that we may gain a heart of wisdom."

— *Psalm 90:12 (NIV)*

Day 277

Affirmation:

I AM DRAGONFLY, faithful to steward what God has entrusted to me for His glory.

Scripture:

"Well done, good and faithful servant!"

— *Matthew 25:21 (NIV)*

____

____

____

____

Day 278

Affirmation:

I AM DRAGONFLY, choosing faithfulness in small things, trusting God with the outcome.

Scripture:

"Whoever can be trusted with very little can also be trusted with much."

— *Luke 16:10 (NIV)*

____

____

____

____

Affirmation:

I AM DRAGONFLY, living with hope beyond this life, confident in God's eternal promises.

Scripture:

"Our light and momentary troubles are achieving for us an eternal glory."

— 2 Corinthians 4:17 (NIV)

Affirmation:

I AM DRAGONFLY, standing firm in faith, knowing my labor in the Lord is not in vain.

Scripture:

"Always give yourselves fully to the work of the Lord, because you know that your labor in the Lord is not in vain."

— 1 Corinthians 15:58 (NIV)

Day 281

Affirmation:

I AM DRAGONFLY, living as a light in this world, allowing God's love to be seen through my words and actions.

Scripture:

"You are the light of the world. A town built on a hill cannot be hidden."

— Matthew 5:14 (NIV)

____

____

____

____

Day 282

Affirmation:

I AM DRAGONFLY, choosing love daily, knowing that love is the greatest legacy I can leave behind.

Scripture:

"And now these three remain: faith, hope and love. But the greatest of these is love."

— 1 Corinthians 13:13 (NIV)

____

____

____

____

Day 283

Affirmation:

I AM DRAGONFLY, sowing seeds of kindness and compassion that will continue to grow long after today.

Scripture:

"Let us not become weary in doing good, for at the proper time we will reap a harvest if we do not give up."
— *Galatians 6:9 (NIV)*

____

____

____

____

Day 284

Affirmation:

I AM DRAGONFLY, living intentionally, knowing my faithfulness today can shape the lives of others tomorrow.

Scripture:

"One generation commends your works to another; they tell of your mighty acts."
— *Psalm 145:4 (NIV)*

____

____

____

____

Day 285

Affirmation:

I AM DRAGONFLY, committed to leaving a legacy that points others to God's light, love, and faithfulness.

Scripture:

"Let your light shine before others, that they may see your good deeds and glorify your Father in heaven."
— Matthew 5:16 (NIV)

Day 286

Affirmation:

I AM DRAGONFLY, trusting God to establish the work of my hands for His lasting purposes.

Scripture:

"May the favor of the Lord our God rest on us; establish the work of our hands for us."
— Psalm 90:17 (NIV)

Day 287

Affirmation:

I AM DRAGONFLY, walking faithfully today, knowing my obedience echoes into eternity.

Scripture:

"Whoever does the will of God lives forever."
— *1 John 2:17 (NIV)*

Day 288

Affirmation:

I AM DRAGONFLY, strengthened to endure, trusting God to renew my strength as I wait on Him.

Scripture:

"But those who hope in the Lord will renew their strength."
— *Isaiah 40:31 (NIV)*

Affirmation:

I AM DRAGONFLY, anchored in an unshakable kingdom that will never fade or fail.

Scripture:

"Therefore, since we are receiving a kingdom that cannot be shaken…"

— Hebrews 12:28 (NIV)

Affirmation:

I AM DRAGONFLY, living with courage and hope, confident that God holds my future securely.

Scripture:

"For the Lord is good and his love endures forever."

— Psalm 100:5 (NIV)

Affirmation:

I AM DRAGONFLY, running my race with perseverance, strengthened by the cloud of witnesses before me.

Scripture:

"Let us run with perseverance the race marked out for us."
— *Hebrews 12:1 (NIV)*

Affirmation:

I AM DRAGONFLY, remaining faithful until the end, trusting God's promise of life.

Scripture:

"Be faithful, even to the point of death, and I will give you life as your victor's crown."
— *Revelation 2:10 (NIV)*

Day 293

Affirmation:

I AM DRAGONFLY, confident that my present faithfulness is producing eternal reward.

Scripture:

"Our light and momentary troubles are achieving for us an eternal glory."

— 2 Corinthians 4:17 (NIV)

Day 294

Affirmation:

I AM DRAGONFLY, living each day with purpose, knowing my life is held securely by God.

Scripture:

"In your book were written all the days ordained for me."
— Psalm 139:16 (NIV)

Affirmation:

I AM DRAGONFLY, walking humbly with God, trusting His guidance through every remaining season.

Scripture:

"Walk humbly with your God."

— Micah 6:8 (NIV)

____

____

____

____

Day 296

Affirmation:

I AM DRAGONFLY, choosing faith over fear, confident in God's eternal care.

Scripture:

"So we fix our eyes not on what is seen, but on what is unseen."

— 2 Corinthians 4:18 (NIV)

____

____

____

____

(**Day 297**)

Affirmation:

I AM DRAGONFLY, confident that God's promises will outlast every season of this life.

Scripture:

"The word of the Lord endures forever."

— *1 Peter 1:25 (NIV)*

____

____

____

____

(**Day 298**)

Affirmation:

I AM DRAGONFLY, living with joy and hope, knowing eternity with God awaits me.

Scripture:

"There will be no more death or mourning or crying or pain."

— *Revelation 21:4 (NIV)*

____

____

____

____

Affirmation:

I AM DRAGONFLY, pressing forward with confidence, trusting God to bring my journey to completion.

Scripture:

"He who began a good work in you will carry it on to completion."

— Philippians 1:6 (NIV)

Affirmation:

I AM DRAGONFLY, standing firm in faith, hopeful and secure in God's eternal promises.

Scripture:

"Let us hold unswervingly to the hope we profess, for he who promised is faithful."

— Hebrews 10:23 (NIV)

SECTION VIII

Completion, Hope & Eternal Confidence

Resting in God's finished work

Affirmation:

I AM DRAGONFLY, resting confidently in the Lord, knowing He is my dwelling place in every season of life.

Scripture:

"Lord, you have been our dwelling place throughout all generations."

— Psalm 90:1 (NIV)

____

____

____

____

Affirmation:

I AM DRAGONFLY, secure in God's unfailing love, which surrounds me now and forever.

Scripture:

"Because your love is better than life, my lips will glorify you."

— Psalm 63:3 (NIV)

____

____

____

____

Day 303

Affirmation:

I AM DRAGONFLY, confident that the Lord watches over my life with care and faithfulness.

Scripture:

"The Lord watches over you—the Lord is your shade at your right hand."

— *Psalm 121:5 (NIV)*

Day 304

Affirmation:

I AM DRAGONFLY, at peace in God's presence, trusting Him to quiet my soul.

Scripture:

"I have calmed and quieted myself."

— *Psalm 131:2 (NIV)*

Affirmation:

I AM DRAGONFLY, rejoicing in the Lord always, allowing His joy to sustain my heart.

Scripture:

"Rejoice in the Lord always. I will say it again: Rejoice!"
— *Philippians 4:4 (NIV)*

Affirmation:

I AM DRAGONFLY, living in hope, confident that God's promises are sure and unchanging.

Scripture:

"For no matter how many promises God has made, they are 'Yes' in Christ."
— *2 Corinthians 1:20 (NIV)*

Affirmation:

I AM DRAGONFLY, strengthened by the Lord's joy, which renews my spirit daily.

Scripture:

"The joy of the Lord is your strength."

— *Nehemiah 8:10 (NIV)*

Affirmation:

I AM DRAGONFLY, confident that God is near, surrounding me with peace and comfort.

Scripture:

"The Lord is near to all who call on him."

— *Psalm 145:18 (NIV)*

Day 309

Affirmation:

I AM DRAGONFLY, resting in the assurance that God's goodness follows me all the days of my life.

Scripture:

"Surely your goodness and love will follow me all the days of my life."

— Psalm 23:6 (NIV)

____

____

____

____

Day 310

Affirmation:

I AM DRAGONFLY, filled with peace and hope as I trust fully in the God of all comfort.

Scripture:

"May the God of hope fill you with all joy and peace as you trust in him."

— Romans 15:13 (NIV)

____

____

____

____

Day 311

Affirmation:

I AM DRAGONFLY, living each day with gratitude, recognizing God's faithfulness in my life.

Scripture:

"Give thanks to the Lord, for he is good; his love endures forever."

— Psalm 107:1 (NIV)

Day 312

Affirmation:

I AM DRAGONFLY, confident that the Lord upholds me and sustains me in every moment.

Scripture:

"The Lord upholds all who fall and lifts up all who are bowed down."

— Psalm 145:14 (NIV)

Day 313

Affirmation:

I AM DRAGONFLY, resting in God's eternal care, free from fear and full of peace.

Scripture:

"Do not let your hearts be troubled and do not be afraid."
— *John 14:27 (NIV)*

Day 314

Affirmation:

I AM DRAGONFLY, confident that my life is hidden with Christ, secure now and forever.

Scripture:

"For you died, and your life is now hidden with Christ in God."

— *Colossians 3:3 (NIV)*

(**Day 315**)

Affirmation:

I AM DRAGONFLY, living in confident rest, trusting God to bring my journey to a beautiful completion.

Scripture:

"The Lord will fulfill his purpose for me."

— Psalm 138:8 (NIV)

____

____

____

____

(**Day 316**)

Affirmation:

I AM DRAGONFLY, celebrating the faithfulness of God, who has walked with me through every season of my life.

Scripture:

"The Lord has done it this very day; let us rejoice today and be glad."

— Psalm 118:24 (NIV)

____

____

____

____

Day 317

Affirmation:

I AM DRAGONFLY, confident that God's goodness and mercy pursue me continually.

Scripture:

"Surely your goodness and love will follow me all the days of my life."

— *Psalm 23:6 (NIV)*

Day 318

Affirmation:

I AM DRAGONFLY, rejoicing in the Lord's salvation, standing secure in His grace.

Scripture:

"The joy of the Lord is your strength."

— *Nehemiah 8:10 (NIV)*

Affirmation:

I AM DRAGONFLY, assured that nothing can separate me from the love of God in Christ Jesus.

Scripture:

"Nothing… will be able to separate us from the love of God that is in Christ Jesus our Lord."

— Romans 8:39 (NIV)

Day 320

Affirmation:

I AM DRAGONFLY, living with bold confidence, knowing the Lord is my light and salvation.

Scripture:

"The Lord is my light and my salvation—whom shall I fear?"

— Psalm 27:1 (NIV)

Affirmation:

I AM DRAGONFLY, strengthened and encouraged, knowing God has been faithful to every promise.

Scripture:

"Not one of all the Lord's good promises… failed; every one was fulfilled."

— Joshua 21:45 (NIV)

Affirmation:

I AM DRAGONFLY, filled with confidence and peace, trusting God with my present and future.

Scripture:

"May the God of hope fill you with all joy and peace as you trust in him."

— Romans 15:13 (NIV)

Day 323

Affirmation:

I AM DRAGONFLY, rejoicing in hope, patient in every season, and faithful in prayer.

Scripture:

"Be joyful in hope, patient in affliction, faithful in prayer."
— *Romans 12:12 (NIV)*

Day 324

Affirmation:

I AM DRAGONFLY, confident that my future is secure in God's loving hands.

Scripture:

"In your book were written all the days ordained for me."
— *Psalm 139:16 (NIV)*

Affirmation:

I AM DRAGONFLY, celebrating the peace God has given me, which guards my heart and mind.

Scripture:

"And the peace of God… will guard your hearts and your minds in Christ Jesus."

— Philippians 4:7 (NIV)

Day 326

Affirmation:

I AM DRAGONFLY, rejoicing in God's presence, confident that He is always near.

Scripture:

"The Lord is near to all who call on him."

— Psalm 145:18 (NIV)

Day 327

Affirmation:

I AM DRAGONFLY, living in joyful assurance, knowing my life is held securely by God.

Scripture:

"No one will snatch them out of my hand."

— John 10:28 (NIV)

Day 328

Affirmation:

I AM DRAGONFLY, praising God for the transformation He has accomplished in my life.

Scripture:

"Give praise to the Lord, proclaim his name; make known among the nations what he has done."

— Psalm 105:1 (NIV)

Affirmation:

I AM DRAGONFLY, standing strong in faith, confident in God's eternal promises.

Scripture:

"Let us hold unswervingly to the hope we profess, for he who promised is faithful."

— Hebrews 10:23 (NIV)

Affirmation:

I AM DRAGONFLY, rejoicing in the assurance that my journey with God continues into eternity.

Scripture:

"Surely I am with you always, to the very end of the age."
— Matthew 28:20 (NIV)

Day 331

Affirmation:

I AM DRAGONFLY, resting in the assurance that God has carried me faithfully through this journey.

Scripture:

"The Lord will watch over your coming and going both now and forevermore."

— *Psalm 121:8 (NIV)*

Day 332

Affirmation:

I AM DRAGONFLY, confident that God's goodness has followed me through every season of my life.

Scripture:

"Surely your goodness and love will follow me all the days of my life."

— *Psalm 23:6 (NIV)*

Day 333

Affirmation:

I AM DRAGONFLY, strengthened by gratitude as I remember all the Lord has done for me.

Scripture:

"Give thanks to the Lord, for he is good; his love endures forever."

— Psalm 107:1 (NIV)

____

____

____

____

Day 334

Affirmation:

I AM DRAGONFLY, standing firm in faith, knowing God has been faithful to every promise.

Scripture:

"Not one of all the Lord's good promises… failed; every one was fulfilled."

— Joshua 21:45 (NIV)

____

____

____

____

Day 335

Affirmation:

I AM DRAGONFLY, living with confidence and peace, trusting God with all that lies ahead.

Scripture:

"May the God of hope fill you with all joy and peace as you trust in him."

— Romans 15:13 (NIV)

____

____

____

____

Day 336

Affirmation:

I AM DRAGONFLY, secure in God's love, knowing nothing can separate me from Him.

Scripture:

"Nothing… will be able to separate us from the love of God that is in Christ Jesus our Lord."

— Romans 8:39 (NIV)

____

____

____

____

Affirmation:

I AM DRAGONFLY, rejoicing in the Lord's presence, which fills my life with peace and joy.

Scripture:

"The Lord is near to all who call on him."

— Psalm 145:18 (NIV)

Affirmation:

I AM DRAGONFLY, living each day with purpose, aware that God orders my steps.

Scripture:

"The Lord makes firm the steps of the one who delights in him."

— Psalm 37:23 (NIV)

Day 339

Affirmation:

I AM DRAGONFLY, confident that my life is held securely in God's faithful hands.

Scripture:

"No one will snatch them out of my hand."

— John 10:28 (NIV)

Day 340

Affirmation:

I AM DRAGONFLY, praising God for the transformation He has accomplished within me.

Scripture:

"Give praise to the Lord, proclaim his name."

— Psalm 105:1 (NIV)

Day 341

Affirmation:

I AM DRAGONFLY, filled with peace as I rest in God's perfect care.

Scripture:

"You will keep in perfect peace those whose minds are steadfast, because they trust in you."

— *Isaiah 26:3 (NIV)*

Day 342

Affirmation:

I AM DRAGONFLY, confident that God's plans for me are good and full of hope.

Scripture:

"For I know the plans I have for you… plans to give you hope and a future."

— *Jeremiah 29:11 (NIV)*

Day 343

Affirmation:

I AM DRAGONFLY, rejoicing in the joy of the Lord, which remains my strength.

Scripture:

"The joy of the Lord is your strength."

— Nehemiah 8:10 (NIV)

Day 344

Affirmation:

I AM DRAGONFLY, trusting God to complete every good work He has begun in me.

Scripture:

"He who began a good work in you will carry it on to completion."

— Philippians 1:6 (NIV)

Day 345

Affirmation:

I AM DRAGONFLY, walking forward with hope, faith, and quiet confidence in God.

Scripture:

"May your unfailing love be my comfort."

— Psalm 119:76 (NIV)

Day 346

Affirmation:

I AM DRAGONFLY, living securely under God's blessing and favor.

Scripture:

"The Lord bless you and keep you."

— Numbers 6:24 (NIV)

Day 347

Affirmation:

I AM DRAGONFLY, confident that the Lord shines His face upon me with grace.

Scripture:

"The Lord make his face shine on you and be gracious to you."

— Numbers 6:25 (NIV)

Day 348

Affirmation:

I AM DRAGONFLY, living in God's peace, upheld by His presence.

Scripture:

"The Lord turn his face toward you and give you peace."
— Numbers 6:26 (NIV)

Day 349

Affirmation:

I AM DRAGONFLY, walking confidently into each new day God has prepared for me.

Scripture:

"This is the day the Lord has made; let us rejoice and be glad in it."

— *Psalm 118:24 (NIV)*

Day 350

Affirmation:

I AM DRAGONFLY, living with assurance, knowing God is with me always.

Scripture:

"Surely I am with you always, to the very end of the age."

— *Matthew 28:20 (NIV)*

Day 351

Affirmation:

I AM DRAGONFLY, anchored in hope that carries me confidently into the future.

Scripture:

"We have this hope as an anchor for the soul, firm and secure."

— *Hebrews 6:19 (NIV)*

Day 352

Affirmation:

I AM DRAGONFLY, rejoicing in eternal life through Christ Jesus my Lord.

Scripture:

"The gift of God is eternal life in Christ Jesus our Lord."

— *Romans 6:23 (NIV)*

Day 353

Affirmation:

I AM DRAGONFLY, walking in freedom, joy, and peace through the Spirit of God.

Scripture:

"Where the Spirit of the Lord is, there is freedom."
— 2 Corinthians 3:17 (NIV)

Day 354

Affirmation:

I AM DRAGONFLY, confident that my life has meaning, purpose, and eternal value.

Scripture:

"For we are God's handiwork."
— Ephesians 2:10 (NIV)

Day 355

Affirmation:

I AM DRAGONFLY, living fully in the love God has poured into my heart.

Scripture:

"God's love has been poured out into our hearts."

— Romans 5:5 (NIV)

Day 356

Affirmation:

I AM DRAGONFLY, resting joyfully in the promise of eternity with God.

Scripture:

"There will be no more death or mourning or crying or pain."

— Revelation 21:4 (NIV)

Day 357

Affirmation:

I AM DRAGONFLY, confident that my journey continues with God beyond this life.

Scripture:

"We will be with the Lord forever."
— 1 Thessalonians 4:17 (NIV)

Day 358

Affirmation:

I AM DRAGONFLY, living each moment with peace, knowing my future is secure in God.

Scripture:

"My sheep listen to my voice… and they follow me."
— John 10:27 (NIV)

Day 359

Affirmation:

I AM DRAGONFLY, praising God for His faithfulness that endures forever.

Scripture:

"His love endures forever."

— Psalm 136:1 (NIV)

____

____

____

____

Day 360

Affirmation:

I AM DRAGONFLY, living with hope that transcends this world.

Scripture:

"Set your hearts on things above."

— Colossians 3:1 (NIV)

____

____

____

____

Day 361

Affirmation:

I AM DRAGONFLY, standing firm in faith until the end.

Scripture:

"Be faithful, even to the point of death."

— Revelation 2:10 (NIV)

Day 362

Affirmation:

I AM DRAGONFLY, rejoicing in the victory given to me through Christ.

Scripture:

"He gives us the victory through our Lord Jesus Christ."

— 1 Corinthians 15:57 (NIV)

Day 363

Affirmation:

I AM DRAGONFLY, confident that my life glorifies God.

Scripture:

"Let your light shine before others."

— Matthew 5:16 (NIV)

Day 364

Affirmation:

I AM DRAGONFLY, resting in God's eternal peace and presence.

Scripture:

"The Lord is my shepherd, I lack nothing."

— Psalm 23:1 (NIV)

Day 365

Affirmation:

I AM DRAGONFLY, transformed, whole, and complete in Christ, forever held in God's love.

Scripture:

"Now to him who is able to do immeasurably more than all we ask or imagine."

— Ephesians 3:20 (NIV)

The **Dragonfly Series** is a multi-book inspirational collection built around the powerful symbolism of the dragonfly—an ancient emblem of **transformation, endurance, faith, renewal, and the courage to rise above adversity**.

Across each title, the dragonfly represents the human journey itself: beginning in darkness, shaped through struggle, and ultimately emerging into freedom, strength, and purpose. Together, the series offers readers emotional healing, spiritual encouragement, creative expression, and personal growth tools that meet them exactly where they are in life.

Each book stands alone while also contributing to an overarching message:

No matter where you begin, transformation is always possible.

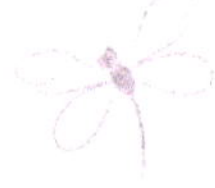

Throughout the series, readers are guided through:

- **Transformation through adversity**

- **Personal renewal and self-discovery**

- **Faith-based hope and spiritual resilience**

- **Mindfulness, creativity, and emotional restoration**

- **The beauty of change rather than fear of it**

- **Learning to rise after seasons of struggle**

The Dragonfly Series speaks to individuals who have experienced:

- trauma or loss

- major life transitions

- burnout or emotional exhaustion

- spiritual questioning

- personal setbacks

- a longing to rediscover purpose and peace

The books gently affirm that **growth is not instant—but it is inevitable when faith, reflection, and intention take flight.**

Life Is Better With Wings: Fly Like a Dragonfly

This adult coloring book serves as the entry point into the Dragonfly Series and introduces readers to the central metaphor of wings as freedom, creativity, and possibility. Designed to inspire calm and clarity, the book features:

- Intricate dragonfly illustrations
- Motivational sayings and affirmations
- Patterns that encourage mindfulness and relaxation

As readers color each page, they are invited into moments of:

- stress relief
- reflection
- emotional grounding
- creative self-expression

The dragonfly becomes a reminder that life does not have to feel heavy—**there is beauty in slowing down, breathing deeply, and allowing creativity to restore the soul.**

This book is not simply artistic; it functions as a **mindfulness tool** that helps readers reconnect with joy, imagination, and inner peace.

Wings of Change: The Beauty of Transformation

This therapeutic coloring book expands the symbolism by walking readers through the **actual life cycle of the dragonfly**—from water-bound nymph to airborne beauty. Each stage mirrors the human experience:

- beginnings that feel unseen

- seasons of waiting

- moments of struggle beneath the surface

- and finally, emergence into something new

The illustrations and themes emphasize:

- patience during change

- resilience during uncertainty

- hope during transition

As readers color, they are encouraged to reflect on their own transformation and recognize that **every stage of growth has value**, even the ones that feel stagnant or painful. "Wings of Change" gently reinforces that **metamorphosis is not loss—it is becoming.**

Dragonfly: Faith in Flight — Where Faith Takes Flight

This deeply inspirational Christian title brings faith to the forefront of the Dragonfly Series.
Blending:

- personal testimony
- biblical principles
- spiritual reflection

the book explores how faith can sustain and strengthen individuals during life's most difficult seasons.

Key spiritual themes include:

- trusting God's plan when answers are unclear
- finding strength through scripture and prayer
- enduring hardship with grace
- allowing God to transform pain into purpose

Readers are reminded that faith does not remove storms—but it gives wings to rise above them.

This book speaks powerfully to believers navigating:

- grief
- disappointment
- unanswered prayers
- spiritual fatigue
- moments when heaven feels silent

"Dragonfly: Faith in Flight" serves as both encouragement and reminder that **God's transformative power is always at work—even when unseen.**

Dragonfly: Where Change Takes Flight

This title focuses on **personal empowerment and resilience**, guiding readers through the process of rebuilding after setbacks.

Through storytelling and reflective insight, the book helps readers:

- understand change as a catalyst rather than a threat

- turn adversity into strength

- identify inner resilience

- release limiting beliefs

- step confidently into new beginnings

It emphasizes that setbacks are not the end of the story— but often the very moment transformation begins.

Readers are encouraged to:

- embrace growth

- heal forward

- redefine their identity beyond past failures

- believe again in possibility

This book reinforces the series' central truth:

You are not broken—you are becoming.

The Collective Impact of the Dragonfly Series

Together, the Dragonfly Series creates a layered and holistic reader experience:

- **Creativity** through coloring and design
- **Emotional healing** through reflection
- **Spiritual growth** through faith-based guidance
- **Personal empowerment** through mindset transformation

The series is intentionally accessible, gentle, and uplifting—never preachy, never overwhelming—making it ideal for:

- readers seeking hope
- individuals in recovery or transition
- faith-based audiences
- self-help and inspirational markets
- gift buyers
- wellness and mindfulness communities

At its heart, the Dragonfly Series delivers one enduring message:

Transformation does not happen all at once—but when the time comes, you will rise.

Like the dragonfly itself, readers are reminded that even after long seasons beneath the surface, **wings are forming**—and when they emerge, they are stronger, freer, and more beautiful than before.